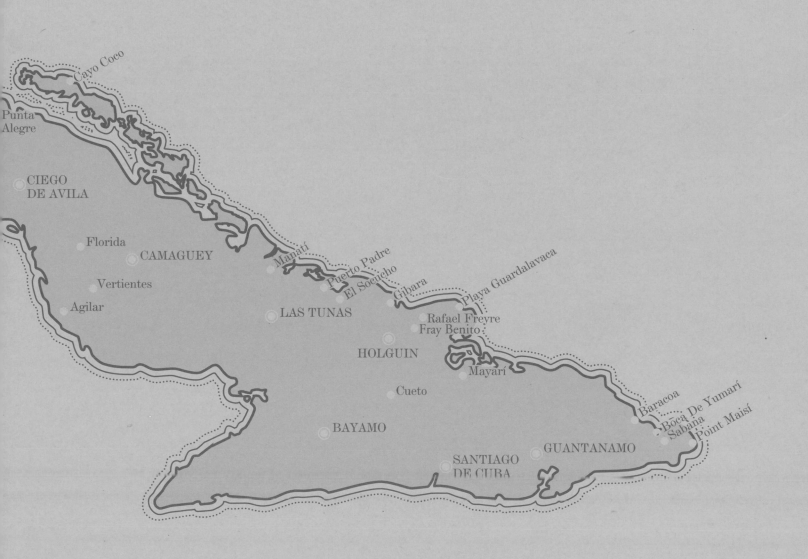

Cayo Coco

Punta
Alegre

CIEGO
DE AVILA

Florida

CAMAGUEY

Manatí

Vertientes

Puerto Padre

El Socucho

Gibara

Playa Guardalavaca

Agilar

LAS TUNAS

Rafael Freyre
Fray Benito

HOLGUIN

Mayarí

Cueto

Baracoa

Boca De Yumarí
Sabana
Point Maisí

BAYAMO

GUANTANAMO

SANTIAGO
DE CUBA

CUBA

LA ISLA ILUSIVA

THE ELUSIVE ISLAND

PHOTOGRAPHS BY TRIA GIOVAN

With excerpts selected by Marilú Menéndez

CUBA

THE ELUSIVE ISLAND
LA ISLA ILUSIVA

HARRY N. ABRAMS, INC., PUBLISHERS
in association with
COMMONPLACE BOOKS

A hummingbird has told me, beautiful Maria,
that they are all still laden with orange blossoms
the sad — oh! — the magical palm trees
in my beautiful homeland.

Me ha dicho un colibrí, linda María
que están todos colgados de azahares
los tristes, ¡ay! los mágicos palmares
en mi patria bella todavía.

JOSE MARTI. Untitled poem. From *Versos sencillos*, 1891.
A journalist, essayist, poet, revolutionary leader, and soldier who is considered the "Apostle of Cuba," José Martí
was the driving force behind the Cuban struggle for independence from Spain. The *Versos sencillos*,
written in exile, capture intimate memories of Martí's youth in Cuba.

DEDICATION

Para mi familia cubana
For my Cuban family

Editors: Spencer Beck, Elisa Urbanelli
Designer: Samuel N. Antupit

Library of Congress Cataloging-in-Publication Data

Giovan, Tria.
Cuba: the Elusive Island: photographs / by Tria Giovan.
p.   cm.
ISBN 0–8109–4042–6 (clothbound)
1. Cuba—Pictorial works. 2. Cuba—Description and travel.
I. Title.
F1765.3.G56 1996
972.9106'4—dc20   96–11527

Published in 1996 by Harry N. Abrams, Incorporated, New York
A Times Mirror Company

FOREWORD

TRIA GIOVAN

I became interested in traveling to Cuba as an outcome of spending my childhood in the Caribbean. An island in such close proximity, yet so inaccessible, and so unlike other familiar places was intriguing and appealing.

My first trip to Cuba was in 1990. The diverse architecture of a sultry Havana, the enigmatic landscapes of the villages and countryside, and the people's openness and warmth all combined for an intense and visually compelling introduction. With a sense of urgency, I returned to photograph this elusive island eight times over the next five years. At the same time, I became engrossed in Cuba's literature, history, and current events.

Exploring the island, developing relationships, and witnessing extraordinary changes was stimulating and enlightening, as well as disheartening and disturbing. Against intricate and often melancholy backdrops, the subtleties and complexities of the day-to-day Cuba were what I was drawn to photograph.

Fully aware of the complex political and emotional issues that surround Cuba, I tread lightly. It has never been my intention to contribute to the pain and disappointment that for many are inextricably tied to this place. I can only hope that these images will enhance, documentarily, Cuba's rich history, and perhaps widen perceptions beyond the realm of political rhetoric.

PROFESION DE FE

Confession of Faith

Creo en el cielo azul: (azul y cielo)
Creo en la tierra humilde, en el precioso
don de la tierra tibia y fuerte
de la tierra bella.

I believe in the blue sky: (blue and sky)
I believe in the humble earth, in the precious
gift from the warm, strong earth,
from the beautiful earth.

DULCE MARIA LOYNAZ. "Profesión de fe." From *Antología lírica*. María Asunción Mateo, ed. Spain: Espasa Calpe, 1993. The daughter of a general in the War of Independence, the poet Dulce María Loynaz won the distinguished Premio Miguel de Cervantes award in 1992. She lives in Cuba.

Father and Daughters on the Malecón, Havana
January 1993

View from Bridge, Sagua la Grande
July 1992

Interior, Remedios
June 1992

11

Man and Oxen, Holguín Province
July 1992

Playing Baseball, Central Havana
January 1996

SON DEL CUBANO TRISTE

Sound of the Sad Cuban

Que no te veré más	That I won't see you again
que no te veré	that I won't see you
que no	that I won't
no.	won't.
Que no te me perderás	That I won't lose you
en el recuerdo,	in my memory,
que no te veré más	that I won't see you again
que no	that I won't
no.	won't.
Que te me vas . . .	That you leave me . . .
Que te me vas . . .	That you leave me . . .
Que te me vas entera.	That you leave me all.
Que la tierra caliente	That the hot earth
Que deberá cubrirme un día	That should cover me one day
se me hace sombra.	is, instead, a shadow.
Que te me esfumas.	That you fade away. . .
¡Oh línea gris de sombra verde!	Oh, gray line of the green shadow!
Que no te veré más	That I won't see you again
que no te veré	that I won't see you
que no	that I won't
no.	won't.

JULIO HERNANDEZ MIYARES. "Son del cubano triste." From *Antillana rotunda.* Barcelona: Editorial Vosgos, 1974. A Cuban poet and academic, Julio Hernández Miyares is the chairman of the Foreign Language Department at Kingsborough College, the City University of New York. The triangular arrangement of verses in his "Son del cubano triste" suggests the Cuban flag.

Portrait in Styrofoam Frame,
Ciego de Avila
January 1993 **15**

Chevrolet in Regla, Havana
January 1992

Barber Shop,
Santiago de Cuba
December 1991

Che Playing Chess, Cultural Center, Mantanzas
January 1993

Woman Waiting in Polyclinic, Molguba
January 1995

Women and Dog in Vedado, Havana
January 1995

Movie Theater, Remedios
July 1992

"Pero en La Habana había luces dondequiera, no sólo útiles sino de adorno, sobre todo en el Paseo del Prado y a lo largo del Malecón, el extendido paseo por el litoral, cruzado por raudos autos que iluminaban veloces la pista haciendo brillar el asfalto, mientras las luces de las aceras cruzaban la calle para bañar el muro, marea luminosa que contrastaban las olas invisibles al otro lado: luces dondequiera, en las calles y en las aceras, sobre los techos, dando un brillo satinado, una pátina luminosa a las cosas más nimias, haciéndolas relevantes, concediéndoles una importancia teatral o destacando un palacio que por día se revelaría como un edificio feo y vulgar."

"But in Havana there were lights everywhere, not only utilitarian ones but decorative, too, especially on the Paseo del Prado and along the Malecón, the expansive avenue along the coast, crisscrossed by speeding cars that swiftly illuminated the roadway, making the asphalt shine, while the lights from the sidewalks crossed the street to bathe the seawall, a luminous tide against the invisible waves on the other side: lights everywhere, on the streets and on the sidewalks, above the rooftops, giving all of it a satiny sheen, a glittering patina to the most trivial things, making them relevant, giving them a theatrical importance or making a palace out of what during the day would reveal itself to be just another ugly and vulgar building."

GUILLERMO CABRERA INFANTE. From *La Habana para un infante difunto (Infante's Inferno)*. Barcelona: Editorial Seix Barral, 1979. One of Cuba's most distinguished writers and critics, Guillermo Cabrera Infante came of age with the Revolution. Eventually designated as an "enemy of the people," he has lived in exile in London since 1965.

El Malecón, Havana

January 1994

Beauty Salon in Vedado, Havana
July 1993

Optica, Caibarién
July 1992

Street with Decorations, Santiago de Cuba
August 1991

Interior with Che and Camilo,
Trinidad
April 1990   **27**

Shoe Repair, Cueto
July 1993

"Por tradición familiar, de quinta generación cubana, me siento ligado a las fuerzas cósmicas del pueblo. Nunca he confundido pueblo y gobierno. En Cuba el pueblo posee virtudes tan poderosas y esenciales que lo hacen destacarse en el concierto humano; entre ellas, destacaría como paradigmáticas la paciencia y la generosidad. . . . Afirmo que los gobiernos nunca han representado a nuestro pueblo. Los gobiernos se han aprovechado de su paciencia y de su generosidad."

"By family tradition, fifth-generation Cuban, I feel attached to the cosmic forces of the Cuban people. I have never mistaken the government for the people. Powerful virtues make Cubans stand out in the concert of humanity; among them I would point out as paradigmatic patience and generosity. . . . I believe that no government has ever represented our people. All governments have, instead, taken advantage of that patience and generosity."

JOSE TRIANA. From "Escritura de la memoria." In *Cuba: La isla posible*. Barcelona: Centre de Cultura Contemporania de Barcelona, 1995. The noted Cuban playwright José Triana is best known for his controversial *La noche de los asesinos*. He lives and works in exile in Paris.

Selling Refrescos, Rafael Freyre
July 1993

Coffee, Bayamo
April 1990

Paseo del Prado y Neptuno, Havana
January 1993

Medicinal Herbs for Sale,
Santiago de Cuba
December 1991

33

"A veces se le sacrifica un cerdo a un Oricha, pero jamás sin consultar previamente al Adivino o sin que lo pida el propio Oricha: su sangre es muy caliente y su organismo, se nos dice, se asemeja al del hombre. . . . En la Regla Kimbisa se sacrifica el cerdo. Se le baña, se le purifica, se le trazan las cruces, y acariciándolo se le conduce ante la Piedra y se le mata."

"Sometimes you sacrifice a pig to an Orisha [Afro-Cuban deity], but never without previously consulting the Priest or without the Orisha himself asking for it: its blood is very hot and its physiology, we are told, similar to that of a man's. . . . According to the Laws of Kimbisa, the pig is sacrificed. It is bathed, it is purified, it is traced with crosses, and, caressing it, it is taken to the Stone and killed."

LYDIA CABRERA. From *Los animales en el folklore y la magia de Cuba*. Miami: Ediciones Universal, 1988. Sister-in-law and disciple of the Cuban anthropologist Fernando Ortiz, Lydia Cabrera invented "anthropoetry" and was one of the first ethnologists/folklorists to explore the roots of African cultures and religions in Cuba. She died in exile in Miami in her nineties.

New Year's Eve Day in Agilar, Camagüey Province
December 1991

Street, Santiago de Cuba
August 1991

Interior with Portrait of
Fidel Castro,
Baracoa
June 1992   37

ESTAMOS

We Are

Estás
haciendo
cosas:
música,
chirimbolos de repuesto,
libros,
hospitales,
pan,
días llenos de propósitos,
flotas,
vida con pocos materiales.

A veces
se diría
que no puedes llegar hasta mañana,
y de pronto
uno pregunta y sí,
hay cine,
apagones,
lámparas que resucitan,
calle mojada por la maravilla,
ojo del alba,
Juan
y cielo de regreso.

Hay cielo hacia adelante.
Todo va saliendo más o menos
bien o mal, o peor,
pero se llena el hueco,
se salta,
sigues,
estás haciendo
un esfuerzo conmovedor con tu pobreza
pueblo mío,
y hasta horribles carnavales, y hasta
feas vidrieras, y hasta
luna.

Repiten los programas,
no hay perfumes,
(adoro esa repetición, ese perfume):
no hay, no hay, pero resulta que
hay.

Estás, quiero decir;
estamos.

You are
making
things:
music,
spare parts,
books,
hospitals,
bread,
days full of purpose,
fleets,
life with few resources.

Sometimes
I would tell you
that you couldn't make it till tomorrow,
and suddenly
one asks and yes,
there are movies,
blackouts,
lamps that resuscitate,
a street wet by wonder,
the eye of the dawn,
Juan
and the returning sky.

There is a sky for tomorrow.
Everything turns out more or less
well or badly, or worse,
but one fills the hole,
one jumps,
you continue,
you are making
a moving effort with your poverty,
my people,
and even horrible carnivals, and even
ugly store windows, and even
the moon.

They repeat the same programs,
there is no perfume,
(I adore that repetition, that perfume):
there is nothing, *no hay*, but it turns out that
there is.

You are here, I mean to say,
we are.

CINTIO VITIER. "Estamos." From *Testimonios*. Havana:
Ediciones UNEAC, 1968. Cintio Vitier, a well-known Cuban writer and literary critic, is the scion of an
illustrious family of Cuban intellectuals spanning three generations. He remains in Cuba.

Food Concession in Vedado, Havana
January 1992

Camilo Cienfuegos Poster,
Old Havana
July 1991

". . . Pagué el recibo de la luz y después, tan lentamente, como lo había decidido, acaricié el gatillo del revólver y me pegué un tiro entre las cejas. El cuerpo lo encontrarían dos días después, ya apestando, entre el mosquero que me condenaba al terror de la extinción parcial dentro del equilibrio de la muerte. Yo me fui esa misma noche al aeropuerto de Miami y tomé el primer avión de regreso a Cuba. Esa noche me enteré que los fantasmas cubanos de los cementerios de Miami lo hacían diariamente. Los treinta y nueve que viajábamos de regreso no íbamos a necesitar ni zapatos, ni ropa, ni comida, ni tarjeta de racionamiento, ni electricidad, ni nada. Nos esperaba sólo La Habana, con empleados socialistas en mangas cortas y sonrisas moriscas auspiciadas por la absoluta carencia de esperanza. Allí en la ciudad que tanto habían disfrutado mis abuelos antes de sus muertes, deambularíamos eternamente entre los leones de El Prado, el sonido del arrecife, el calor agotador de las tardes de agosto, las lunas de mayo, los fríos de diciembre, con todos los demás espíritus que como en mi niñez llenaban las noches habaneras; esta vez sabría Dios, o Lezama, hasta cuando. . . ."

". . . I paid the light bill and then, slowly, as I had planned it, caressed the gun's trigger and shot myself between the eyes. The body would be found two days later, already smelling, among the flies that condemned me to the terror of partial extinction within the stillness of death. That same night, I went to the Miami airport and took the first flight back to Cuba. That night I found out that Cuban ghosts of the Miami cemeteries did it every day. The thirty-nine returning that night were going to need no shoes, no clothes, no food, no ration card, no electricity, no anything. The only thing that awaited us was Havana, with its socialist employees in shirtsleeves sporting those Moorish smiles that proclaim an absolute lack of hope. There, in the city that my grandparents had so enjoyed before their deaths, we would walk for all eternity among the lions in El Prado, the sound of the waves against the reef, the exhausting August sun, the May moons, the cold days of December, amidst all the other spirits that, as in my childhood, filled the nights of Havana: this time, only God, or Lezama, knew for how long. . . ."

MANUEL CACHAN. From "Volverán las oscuras golondrinas." In *Apuntes Postmodernos*. José A. Solis, ed. Miami, 1995. Manuel Cachan is an award-winning Cuban writer and a professor of literature at the University of Georgia at Valdosta.

Bus Stop and Gran Teatro de la Habana, Havana
January 1994

Casa de la Trova,
Santiago de Cuba
August 1991

44

Coffee Counter, Havana
April 1990

José Martí Statue with Mural,
Santiago de Cuba
46 *August 1991*

VIVIR SIN HISTORIA

To Live without History

He viajado poco, he vivido menos.
No se explica este cansancio y sin embargo,
estoy cansado.

Desde mi margen contemplo
a los hombres pararayos, a los hombres volcán,
a los hombres liebre.
Cotemplo al héroe de última hora
y al mártir del momento.
Contemplo las inmolaciones, los sacrificios,
las bellas catástrofes que harán historia.

Yo no tengo historia
y sin embargo, estoy cansado.

Cansado de la historia entre otras cosas,
y de las inmolaciones y de los sacrificios
y de las bellas catástrofes
y sobre todo de los mártires.
Pudrirse de grima en una cárcel
puede ser mala suerte o mala leche

mas ya cansa tanta tragedia:
tanta viuda atrincherada en su luto,
tanto hijo huérfano,
tanto exilio, tanto padecer.

La orfandad es bonita, pero también cansa.
El dolor de los demás es bonito
pero también cansa.

Atención bayameses:
bajad las voces
detened la marcha
deshizen las banderas
y dejen las bayonetas.

Traigo un secreto que confiaros:
vivir sin historia es vivir.

I have travelled little, I have lived less.
My weariness is hard to explain and yet,
I am tired.

From my corner I contemplate
the lightning-rod men, the volcano men,
the harelike men.
I contemplate the latest hero
and the martyr of the moment.
I contemplate the immolations, the sacrifices,
the beautiful catastrophes that will make history.

I don't have a history,
and yet, I am tired.

Tired of history, among other things,
and of the immolations and of the sacrifices
and of the beautiful catastrophes
and above all of the martyrs.
To rot in jail
could be bad luck or bad karma

but so much tragedy is tiresome:
so many widows steeped in mourning,
so many orphan sons,
such long exile, such suffering.

Orphanhood is beautiful, but it is also tiresome.
Someone else's pain is beautiful
but it is also tiresome.

Listen, people of Bayamo:
lower your voices
stop your march
lower the flags
and leave the bayonets behind.

I have a secret to share with you:
to live without history is to live.

GUSTAVO PEREZ FIRMAT. "Vivir sin historia." From
Equivocaciones. Madrid: Editorial Betania, 1989. A poet, fiction writer, and scholar, Gustavo Pérez Firmat
came to the U.S. at the age of eleven in the wake of Castro's takeover. He is now a professor of Spanish at
Duke University.

Cuban Flag, Cienfuegos
December 1992

Christmas Tree and Election Slogan, Santiago de las Vegas
January 1993

Afternoon in Viñales, Pinar del Río Province
January 1993

VIAJE A LA SEMILLA
Journey to the Source

"Las mantas de lana se destejían, redondeando un vellón de carneros distantes. Los armarios, los bargueños, las camas, los crucifijos, las mesas, las persianas, salieron volando en la noche, buscando sus antiguas raíces al pie de las selvas. Todo lo que tuviera clavos se desmoronaba . . . todo se metamorfoseaba, regresando a la condición primera. El barro volvió al barro, dejando un yermo en lugar de la casa."

"The wool blankets were unraveling, spinning themselves into the fleecy tufts of distant flocks of sheep. The armoires, the big chests, the beds, the crucifixes, the tables, the shutters, all flew away in the night, in search of their ancient roots at the foot of the forest. Everything that was nailed down crumbled . . . everything metamorphosed, returning to its primeval state. Mud became mud again, leaving a barren wasteland in place of the house."

ALEJO CARPENTIER. "Viaje a la semilla." From *Cuentos.* Barcelona: Editorial Laia, 1974. A musicologist, critic, revolutionary, and diplomat, Alejo Carpentier is perhaps Cuba's best-known writer. One of the principal architects of "magical realism" and the so-called New Novel in Latin America, he died in Paris in 1980.

Residential Building in Vedado, Havana
April 1990

Front Desk of Havana Libre Hotel, Havana
January 1993

Woman Waiting,
Central Havana
February 1995   **55**

House of Poet Dulce María Loynaz, Havana
January 1993

Woman Selling
from Stairwell,
Central Havana
January 1994

57

I read my first erotic novel when I was eleven or twelve, in the living room of a boarding house in Santiago de Cuba. We stayed there for a week every year when my family went on a pilgrimage to the shrine of the island's patron saint, the Virgin of Charity, in the old mining town of El Cobre, a few miles from Santiago. The city of Santiago was old and funky, yet prosperous, and of a different tone and cadence than sophisticated, Americanized Havana. Right outside the shutters of the boarding-house living-room windows coursed a beguiling multi-hued culture, part Spanish, part French, part Negro, not unlike New Orleans. While inside that hot shuttered room, poorly cooled by the sultry breeze from a ceiling fan, I discovered the arousal of written narrative, as the novel, a cheap romance with very little sex in it, told of a nun's seduction by some rogue and — this was rich! — her pregnancy. The book was obviously the property of one of the two teenage daughters of the widow who owned the boarding house, or perhaps it belonged to the widow herself, a distraction from provincial boredom and a channel for her longings. Every day at noon, we were served steaming, herb-infused Creole dishes on the terraced floor that ringed the inner patio, and every afternoon, during siesta time, I would retire to my story of seduction overcoming piety and the wages of sin. I grew dizzy reading it. And I never overcame the feeling that it was all of one piece: shuttered living rooms, ceiling fans, inner patios, herbal cooking, the curiosity of adolescent girls, the longings of women who had known men and lost them, a city overflowing with colors and accents, the thrill of seduction, the erotic power of piety, my desire for them all, for it all, my desire.

ENRIQUE FERNANDEZ. November 1995. A journalist and the foremost reviewer of Latin pop culture in America, Enrique Fernández is the editor of *Exito*, a Miami-based Spanish-language weekly.

Three Men, Remedios
January 1993

Group Portrait, Gibara
July 1993

Street in Agilar, Camagüey Province
December 1991

Bohío, Holguín Province
July 1993

Interior in Agilar, Camagüey Province
January 1992

View from El Castillo, Baracoa
June 1991

Woman in Window,
Baracoa
July 1992

". . . These houses are constructed of thin strips of the palm tree or bamboo, with sometimes a fibrous material from the coconut tree perched in between them. The roof is thatched with palm leaves and the floor merely bare ground and that is worn into a rough, uneven condition. There may be partitions dividing the space into several rooms, which seem unusually dark on account of closure of the window-shutter, if there be one. A few rough chairs and a table constitute the furniture, which with some enormous and ornamental saddles, some ox-yokes, and a piece of jerked beef, with small sheafs of unwhittled rice or bunches of herbs hanging from the rafters, make up the household furniture."

RICHARD J. LEWIS.
From *Diary of a Spring Holiday in Cuba*. Philadelphia: Porter and Coates, 1872.

Bohío Interior,
Florida
April 1990   **67**

Poster at Coffee Collective, Lake Habananilla
July 1991

Housewares Store, Bayamo
April 1990

Cafeteria in Vedado, Havana
February 1995

"This House Is the Guard Today," Caibarién
July 1992

Cold Water, Lake Habananilla
July 1991

"It is easy to forget, amid the dramatic images of people risking their lives to flee in makeshift boats, that Cubans have had a crash course in suffering and sacrifice for decades now. They have developed reserves of resourcefulness and patience that would put the rest of us to shame."

PICO IYER. From "Castro's Resilient Masses." *The New York Times*, August 30, 1994. A journalist and writer, Pico Iyer is the author of the novel *Cuba and the Night* (Quartet, 1995). He lives in Santa Barbara, California.

Plaza de la Revolución, Havana
January 1993

Walking on the Malecón, Havana
July 1992

"Havana was a true evening city, radiant, luminous, and mysterious. As dusk arrived, the bright signs on the Malecon lit up, and the larger-than-life neon woman, poised on a rooftop platform in her neon Jantzen bathing suit, dived down the side of a skyscraper. Multicolored stars popped from a huge neon Philco television set, shooting over the dark evening skyline like fireworks. The scene was magical.

The tourists' Havana was a city of pleasure, with a balmy sensuality that affected visitors and natives alike. In the grand hotels like the Nacional, designed by McKim, Mead, and White, every whim was catered to. At the Tropicana nightclub designed by Max Borges Recio, people dined and danced outdoors under the stars and palm trees in the Salon Bajo las Estrellas, while indoors, they dined in Los Arcos de Cristal, an arched salon with walls of glass panels. The Montmartre, an amusing nightclub, was a replica of the Moulin Rouge in Paris. Elegant casinos (under dubious management) lured the high rollers of the international set who gambled until dawn.

Exotic tropical drinks were a part of the tourists' fantasy of Havana, promising glamour and fun. Although some drinks were given American names, like the 'Miami Beach' and the 'Floridita Bronx,' the cocktails enjoyed at bars like Sloppy Joe's and Floridita were typically Cuban, based on rum, sugar, and Caribbean fruits. They may seem overly sweet to our sophisticated tastes, but they were a true reflection of the sweet life that lured so many travelers to Cuba."

MARY URRUTIA RANDELMAN and Joan Schwartz. From *Memories of a Cuban Kitchen*. New York: Macmillan Publishing Company, 1992. Mary Urrutia Randelman was born in Havana and emigrated to the U.S. in 1958. She lives in New York.

Habana Libre Hotel, Havana
January 1994

Coffee Collective Dining Room, Lake Habananilla
July 1991

Man in Marianao, Havana
January 1993

". . . If we turned to an ordinary dictionary for a definition of the *mampara* — 'a folding screen made of a wooden, cloth, or leather frame . . .' — we would get a very inadequate idea of what in reality is one of the more important decorative and architectural elements that transfigured Cuban residences many centuries ago and helped to shape the Cuban lifestyle. The *mampara,* a door truncated to the height of a man, was the real interior door of the Creole home for hundreds of years, creating a peculiar concept of family relations and communal living in general. The classic *mampara* of the Cuban middle class was, in the days of our adolescence, a door superimposed — in terms of the placement of the hinges — on the real door, which was never closed or opened, other than at times of illness or the death of the room's dweller or when, in the winter, *los nortes* — the winds from the north — blew hard . . . . The *mampara* that isolated the residents well enough not to see each other gave rise, in those homes with many children and many family members, to the habit of speaking loudly from one end of the house to the other, thus informing the neighbors of even the pettiest of family conflicts. The problem of 'incommunication,' so often posed by recent novelists was not posed in houses with *mamparas,* whose vibrant glass transmitted any announcement as far back as the intimate shadows of the patio. . . ."

ALEJO CARPENTIER. From *La ciudad de las columnas.* Barcelona: Editorial Lumen, 1970. This excerpt is a marvelous example of the "Cuban baroque" style.

Interior, Trinidad
April 1990

Sabana Bohío, Baracoa
December 1991

Family Portrait in Boyeros, Havana
December 1993

"I can still smell the sweet aromas that emanated from that kitchen and from all the kitchens in the neighborhood. One could almost tell the time of the day by them: the bracing blend of Cuban coffee brewing and raw milk boiling for *café con leche* meant that it was about 7:00 A.M., almost time *para desayunarse,* to eat breakfast. The pungent aroma of sautéing *sofrito*, the mixture of onion, garlic and green bell pepper that is the basis of so many Cuban dishes, meant that noon was near, time for *el almuerzo,* the three-course midday meal. The delicate scent of a sour orange-juice marinade bathing a piece of steak or chicken might signal the approach of *la comida,* the formal evening meal."

MARIA JOSEFA LLURIA DE O'HIGGINS. From *A Taste of Old Cuba.* New York: HarperCollins, 1994. María Josefa Lluriá de O'Higgins left Cuba in her teens to attend boarding school in Philadelphia, but returned each summer until the Communist revolution. Today she lives with her family in Miami.

Lunch in Boyeros, Havana
July 1992

Fighting Fish, Agilar, Camagüey Province
January 1992

Family on Vacation at Playa Blanca, Holguín Province
July 1992

"Pilar looked so clumsy last night dancing with Ivanito. The band was playing a cha-cha-cha, and Pilar moved jerkily, off the beat, sloppy and distracted. She dances like an American. Ivanito, though, is a wonderful dancer. His hips shift evenly, and his feet keep precise time to the music. He glides through his turns as if he were ice-skating.

When Lourdes finally danced with her nephew, she felt beholden to the congas, to a powerful longing to dance. Her body remembered what her mind had forgotten. Suddenly, she wanted to show her daughter the artistry of *true* dancing. Lourdes exaggerated her steps, flawless and lilting, teasing the rhythm seductively. She held the notes in her hips and her thighs, in the graceful arch of her back. Ivanito intuited her movements, dipping her with such reluctant fluidity that the music ached and blossomed around them. The crowd gradually pulled back to watch their unlikely elegance. Then someone clapped, and in an instant the room rumbled with applause as Lourdes spun and spun and spun across the polished dance floor."

CRISTINA GARCIA. From *Dreaming in Cuban*. New York: Alfred A. Knopf, 1992. Born in Cuba, Cristina García emigrated to New York as a young child shortly after Castro's takeover. *Dreaming in Cuban* is her first work of fiction.

Dancing at the Beach, Isabela de Sagua
July 1992

Tea House, Viñales
January 1993

Pineapple Pickers, Ciego de Avila Province
April 1990

Playa de Santa María del Mar, Havana Province
April 1990

Between Varadero and Havana, Mantanzas Province
April 1990

Cane Cutters, Camagüey Province
April 1990

*"La caña insistentemente crece ahí en el caña-
veral es persistente monótona interminable y sólo la violencia puede cortarla sólo la obstina-
ción puede tumbarla sólo la locura puede insistir el cuerpo molido las manos llagadas los
riñones quejándose levanta el machete baja el machete la caña es siempre la misma y el sol pero
primero el rocío por la mañana las botas mojadas caminando por la carretera o en camión o
el tractor por el camino las guardarrayas al amanecer todavía frío aunque no se ve en la oscu-
ridad la caña está ahí se descubren los cañaverales en la sombra de la niebla y se ven eso sí las
cañas al borde del camino y entonces tu surco inmóvil . . . "*

"The cane grows insistently there on the
cañaveral [plantation] it is persistent monotonous endless and only violence can cut it only
obstinancy can knock it down only madness can insist that the worn-out body the hands
full of sores the complaining kidneys bring up the machete bring down the machete the
cane is always the same and the sun but first the dew early in the morning the wet boots
walking along the highway or in the truck or the tractor on the road the *guardarrayas* at
dawn cold still although it cannot be seen in the darkness the cane is there the cane fields
emerge from the shadow of the fog and it can be seen oh yes the cane at the edge of the road
and then your furrow immobile . . . "

EDMUNDO DESNOES. From "Aquí me pongo." In *Los diapos-
itivos en la flor*. Edmundo Desnoes, ed. Hanover, N.H.: Ediciones del Norte, 1981. A Cuban novelist and
essayist who was a part of the revolutionary intelligentsia until 1979, Edmundo Desnoes is the author of
Memories of Underdevelopment and the screenplay for the award-winning film of the same name. He lives
in New York.

Sunday Afternoon, Remedios
January 1993

Zone of Defense, Fray Benito

July 1993

INSTRUCCIONES PARA INGRESAR EN UNA NUEVA SOCIEDAD

Instructions for Entering a New Society

Lo primero: optimista.
Lo segundo: atildado, comedido, obediente.
(Haber pasado todas las pruebas deportivas.)
Y finalmente andar
como lo hace cada miembro:
un paso al frente, y
dos o tres atrás:
pero siempre aplaudiendo.

First: be optimistic.
Second: judgmental, restrained, obedient.
(Having passed every athletic challenge.)
And, finally, walk as every member does:
one step forward, and
two or three backward:
but always applauding.

HEBERTO PADILLA. "Instrucciones para ingresar en una nueva sociedad." From *Fuera del juego*. Buenos Aires: Aditor Publicaciones, 1969. Considered Cuba's foremost living poet, Heberto Padilla won Cuba's National Prize for literature, but was later arrested for the political views expressed in poems such as this. His imprisonment cost Castro the support of many intellectuals in Cuba and abroad. Padilla has lived in exile in Miami since 1980.

Prisoners, Pinar del Río
January 1993

View from the Hotel Colina, Havana
July 26, 1993

Playing Dominoes in Agilar, Camagüey Province
December 1992

House of Poet Dulce María Loynaz, Havana
December 1992

It was always like a party at my grandparents' dining table. We were so many. The family, the friends that came every night because they had no children of their own, and my grandmother couldn't imagine them sitting down to dine alone, those who were invited for that particular evening, and those who happened to show up. The dining room was immense, taking up the entire width of the house, a French door at each end, one opening to the *portal* and the other one to the patio with the rosebushes, their wonderful scent brought to us inside by the warm tropical breeze. It was an elegant room with mahogany-paneled walls, crystal chandeliers, massive silver services, and multicolored Baccarat goblets that now I often see in museums. I don't remember the table, for it was always covered with lace, but I do remember that the chairs had brown leather seats and were not comfortable, although the conversation was so interesting I never minded that they weren't. I don't want to give the impression that those were elegant dinners. No, no. They were loud and intense, everyone talking at the same time, as Cubans do, and there were many lively arguments and many many jokes and pranks. I remember the time my uncle threw a piece of bread to my father across the long table — my grandfather had died by then and each brother headed one side — and how my grandmother almost fainted with embarrassment. There were two nuns and a priest there that night — and not merely a priest, somebody with rank in the Church. I remember the red trim and the rows of little buttons and how he did not take off the small cap perched at the back of his head when he sat down to eat, as men are supposed to do. The nuns were *boquiabiertas*, shocked, but the priest laughed really hard and I could tell he thought we were just being a happy family. Also, the children were allowed to give their opinion about everything at those dinners — which might have been modern, but not elegant, and something of which my other grandmother didn't approve. *"Los niños hablan cuando las gallinas orinan,"* which is *never,* she was always telling us and my father and my uncle, whom she blamed for our brazen behavior, and sometimes now, when I know I have talked too much or sounded too vehement, which is not appreciated here, I think of her and that she might have been right after all and that I should have learned then to keep my thoughts to myself. And the servants, too, often intervened to give their take on things, set the family history straight or tattle on one of us children or on each other. So they were not elegant dinners, those dinners at my grandparents', despite the beauty of the surroundings and the luxury of the accoutrements, they were not elegant at all, not even when we had illustrious company. But the food was exquisite. Out of Susana's kitchen came the most sophisticated dishes of Spanish and French cuisine, sometimes Italian and Chinese, too, all perfectly cooked and beautifully presented, nobody knows how, since she never learned to read a recipe nor lived anywhere else but in her little village in Spain and in my grandmother's house. But no one, except my grandmother herself and perhaps my mother and a few of the guests, seemed to really admire her efforts. What we loved best, all of us, what we wanted always, what we begged for, was Cuban food. The *ropa viejas* and *tasajos* and *moros y cristianos*. And, of course, the highly seasoned pork, the best in the world, and the black beans and rice and the *yuca con mojito* and the fried plantains. We had that every other Sunday and on all the holidays — *Nochebuena, Reyes,* and the *Veinte de Mayo.* We still cook those same things on those days, but here they don't seem to taste the same.

MARILU MENENDEZ, 1996. Marilú Menéndez left Cuba in 1961. A scholar of Latin American history, she lives and works in New York City and is currently writing a memoir.

Chairs, Las Tunis Province
April 1990

Havana Harbor and Casa Blanca, Havana
June 1992

Office with Che and Camilo, Havana
July 1993

Janet at Home in Boyeros, Havana
January 1994

Street, Old Havana
January 1994

LETTER FROM
A TWELVE-YEAR-OLD

"... *Nos fuimos para la parada de la 79, hay una sola ruta ahora, las guaguas están 'inmetibles' por decirles así. Las jabas de nylon son finitas y por ellas se sabe que se fue a comprar a la diplotienda. Vino la guagua y montó a todo el mundo, no cabía más nadie. Yo con mi carácter que a veces soy un dulce, pero otras veces no hay quien me soporte porque protesto por todo ... comencé a protestar que me estaban empujando y eso no me gusta. Estuve apretujada en un lugar como por cinco minutos hasta que al fin pude pasar hacia atrás, y entonces me dí cuenta de que las jabas estaban partidas. Cuando llegamos fui a sacar los refrescos, las maltas y las latas de leche condensada para ponerlas a frío y —¡qué horror!— desaparecieron tres refrescos, las de la malta y mi chocolate que fue lo que más me dolió! ..."*

"... We went to the bus stop, the 79 is the only route now, the *guaguas* [local buses] are 'unboardable,' I guess you could say. The nylon bags are very flimsy and if you carry them everyone knows you have been to the 'diplo'-store. The *guagua* came and everyone went aboard, even though there was no room. Me, with my personality that sometimes is as sweet as candy but other times unbearable, because I complain about everything ... I began to protest that I was being pushed and I don't like that. I was shoved into a corner for about five minutes until I could finally move to the back of the bus, and it was then that I realized that the bags had been broken. When we got home I took out the sodas, the *maltas,* and the cans of condensed milk to put them in the cold and — horrors! — three sodas and the *maltas* had disappeared *and* my chocolate, which is what hurt the most! ..."

JENNIFER HERNANDEZ, June 1995.
Excerpt from a letter sent from Havana to a friend in New York.

Bus Stop, Havana
June 1995   **111**

Coffee Collective Kitchen, Lake Habananilla
July 1991

La Rusa Hotel, Baracoa
December 1991

Diego: ". . . vivimos en una de las ciudades más maravillosas del mundo. Todavía estás a
tiempo de ver algunas cosas antes de que se derrumbe y se la trague la mierda . . ."
David: ". . . Diego, no seas injusto, que son muchas las cosas, una ciudad no se repara . . ."
Diego: "La están dejando caer, eso no me lo discutas . . ."
David: ". . . somos un país pequeño, con todo en contra . . ."
Diego: "Sí pero es como si no les importara, no sufren cuando la ven . . ."
David: ". . . a algunos sí nos importa. A tí y a mí nos importa."

Diego: ". . . we live in one of the most enchanting cities in the world. You still have time to
see some things before she crumbles and is swallowed by all the shit . . ."
David: ". . . Diego, don't be so unjust; there are many problems, a city can't be
repaired . . ."
Diego: "They are allowing her to collapse, don't argue that with me . . ."
David: ". . . we are a little country, with everything against us . . ."
Diego: "Yes, but it is as if she didn't matter to them; they don't suffer when they look
at her . . ."
David: ". . . she matters to some of us. She matters to you and she matters to me."

SENEL PAZ. Dialogue from the film *Fresa y chocolate*
(Strawberries and Chocolate), Miramax Films, 1993. A writer and screenwriter best known for the daring
treatment of homosexuality in his short stories and films, Senel Paz was awarded the prestigious Juan
Rulfo Award in Paris in 1990. *Fresa y chocolate* was nominated for an Oscar in 1995 for Best Foreign Film.
He lives in Cuba.

Exterior in Vedado,
Havana
February 1995   **115**

Woman Grinding Coffee,
River Toa Region, Baracoa
June 1992

At the Beach, Cayo Conuco
July 1992

"And first the climate. Anything more delicious can scarcely be conceived of. It does not smile at you one day and frown at you the next — *aujourd'hui vôtre serviteur, demain, Judas* — after the changeable fashion of our northern summer; but day after day of genial warmth and unclouded splendour unfold before you, more intoxicably sweet and satisfyingly fair as the season advances. The terms 'winter' and 'spring' seem almost to lose their significance in a land always green with verdure, fragrant with bloom and luscious with fruit."

JULIA LOUISA MATILDA CURTISS WOODRUFF. From *My Winter in Cuba*. New York: E. P. Dutton & Co., Hartford Church Press, 1871.

Man Selling Marañones, Point Maisí
June 1992

Cayo Coco, Camagüey Province
January 1993

Man on Horse, El Socucho
July 1993

Abuela, Boyeros, Havana
February 1995

THE NIGHT, MY GRANDMOTHER

"But perhaps even more impressive and mysterious than the morning fog was the night. It would be very difficult for anyone who has not experienced night in the open country to have a clear understanding of the splendors of nature, much less of its mystery. Night was not only infinite space above. Night in the countryside where I grew up (a countryside that no longer exists, except in these recollections) was also a musical realm, a magical and endless orchestration, vibrating everywhere, chiming into infinity. And the sky's radiance was not constant but an unending blaze of changing hues and streaks, stars that burst and disappeared (after having existed for millions of years) just to enrapture us for a few moments.

My grandmother could find the most important stars, and even the lesser-known ones, at any time of night. Whether by sheer instinct or because she had observed the skies for so many years, she could quickly indicate the position of those stars, as well as name them, although the names she gave them were certainly not the ones used by astronomers. For example, they had names like the Cross of May, the Seven Kids, the Plow. There they were, in that immense darkness shining for my grandmother, who would show them to me and not only be able to name them but, in accordance with their position and brightness, forecast the day's weather and also predict the future: whether it would rain the next day; whether the harvest, in two or three months, would be good or bad; whether it would hail; whether the dreaded hurricanes would come. . . . My grandmother would try to drive away hurricanes by making crosses with ashes. When the storm was approaching, she would come with a bucket full of ashes from the stove and spread them in the four corners of the house, throw fistfuls of ashes into the air, and make crosses in the passageway and near the roof supports of the house. In this way she would try to appease the forces of nature.

What literary influence did I have in my childhood? Practically none: no books, no teaching, with the exception of the school assemblies we called 'Kiss to the Homeland.' But regarding the magical, the mysterious, which is so essential for the development of creativity, my childhood was the most literary time of my life. And this I owe, in large measure, to that mythical figure of my grandmother, who would interrupt her housework or throw down her bundle of firewood in the woods and start talking with God.

My grandmother knew the medicinal powers of almost all herbs, and prepared brews and infusions for all kinds of diseases. With a clove of garlic she would take care of indigestion by massaging not the stomach but a leg. By means of a system she called *las cabañuelas,* which consisted of twelve heaps of salt that she would uncover on the first of January, she would forecast the rainy season and the dry season of the year to come.

Night also came under my grandmother's domain; at night she ruled. She understood that family gatherings in the evening acquired a transcendence not readily explainable; she would therefore invite the whole family under any pretext: sweets, coffee, a prayer. Thus, in a circle of candlelight, my grandmother would officiate. Beyond, there was the infinite night of the countryside, but she had created a space against the darkness and was not about to give it up easily. . . ."

REINALDO ARENAS. From "The Night, My Grandmother." In *Before Night Falls.* Translated by Dolores M. Koch. New York: Viking-Penguin Books, 1993. One of the most gifted and unconventional of Cuba's younger generation of writers, Reinaldo Arenas was designated as a counterrevolutionary after the publication of his second novel *(Hallucinations)* in 1968. He had to smuggle much of his subsequent work out of the country. He died in exile in New York in 1990.

Summer Afternoon, Caibarién
July 1992

Cigar Factory, Gibara
July 1993

"El tabaco es cosa hombruna. Sus hojas son vellosas, como trabajadas y oscurecidas al sol, y su color es el de la suciedad . . . el viril tabaco exige manos delicadas, de mujer o de femenina finura para su trato liviano. Antaño los tabacos para la fuma del guajiro veguero eran 'elaborados por su mujer, por su hija o por sus queridas,' como observó la Condesa de Merlin . . . En Cuba es popular la despalilladora y en España la Carmen fue cigarrera."

"Tobacco is a masculine thing. Its leaves are hairy, tanned and darkened by the sun, its color is that of dirt . . . but the virile tobacco demands delicate hands, those of a woman's or those with the feminine exquisiteness necessary for the required light touch. In the old days, the cigars smoked by the tobacco planter were 'rolled by his wife, by his daughter or by his mistresses,' as the Countess of Merlin observed . . . In Cuba, the female tobacco roller is popular, and in Spain, *'la Carmen'* was a cigar maker."

FERNANDO ORTIZ. From *Contrapunteo cubano del tabaco y el azúcar.* Havana: Jesus Montero, 1940. The most distinguished Cuban cultural anthropologist, Fernando Ortiz coined such bywords as "transculturation" and "Afro-Cuban," among others. In this classic treatise, Ortiz equates "tobacco" with all that is native and good in Cuban culture and "sugar" with all that is foreign and bad.

Photograph in Miramar Home, Havana
March 1995

Young Women on the Malecón, Havana
January 1994

129

COMO FUE

How It Happened

Cómo fue . . .
no sé decirte cómo fue,
no sé explicarte qué pasó,
pero de ti me enamoré.
Fue una luz que iluminó
todo mi ser.
Tu risa como un manantial
regó me vida de inquietud.

Fueron tus ojos o tu boca,
fueron tus manos o tu voz;
fue a lo mejor la impaciencia
de tanto esperar
tu llegada.

Mas no sé,
no sé decirte cómo fue,
no sé explicarte qué pasó,
pero de ti me enamoré.

How did it happen . . .
I don't know how to tell you how it did
I don't know how to explain to you what happened,
but I fell in love with you.
It was like a light that illuminated
all my being.
Your laughter, like a spring,
soaked my life with restlessness.

Was it your eyes or your mouth,
was it your hands or your voice;
was it, perhaps, the anticipation,
the thrill of waiting so long
for you to arrive.

But I don't know,
I don't know how to tell you how it happened,
I don't know how to explain to you what happened,
but I fell in love with you.

ERNESTO DUARTE. From *Benny Moré,* by Raúl Martínez Rodríguez. Havana: Editorial Letras Cubanas, 1993. Written by songwriter Ernesto Duarte, this tune was popularized by the celebrated Cuban performer Benny Moré during the 1940s and '50s.

Young Couple, Remedios
January 1993

Fish Tank, Baracoa
December 1991

Landscape near Dimas, Pinar del Río Province
January 1993

Reputed Cross of Christopher Columbus, Baracoa
December 1991

"Esta es la tierra más hermosa que ojos humanos hayan visto . . ." [1]

". . . a la parte del Sur un singularísimo puerto, y de la parte del Sueste unas tierras hermosas a maravilla, así como una vega montuosa dentro de esas montañas . . . la lindeza de la tierra y de los árboles donde hay pinos y palmas, y de la grande vega . . . montes llanos y bajos, la más hermosa cosa del mundo, y salen por ella muchas riberas de aguas que descienden destas montañas . . ." [2]

"This is the most beautiful land that human eyes have ever seen . . ." [1]

". . . to the south a most singular port, and in the southeast the most beautiful landscape, a wonder, also a hilly plain cradled in the mountains . . . the beauty of the land and of the trees, pines and palms, and of the large plain . . . and the rolling hills, the most beautiful thing in the world, and the rivers that descend from these mountains . . ." [2]

CHRISTOPHER COLUMBUS. [1]*The Journal*, entry for October 27, 1492. [2]*The Journal*, entry for November 27, 1492, upon "discovering" Baracoa. From *The Diario of Christopher Columbus's First Voyage to America, 1492–1493*, translated by Oliver Dunn and James E. Kelley, Jr. The University of Oklahoma Press, 1989.

Landscape, Holguín Province
July 1993

Interior in Vedado, Havana
April 1990

Buildings, Gibara
July 1993

Bandstand, Gibara
July 1992

No he de caerme, no, que yo soy fuerte
en vano me embisten los ciclones
y me ha roído el tiempo hueso y carne,
y la humedad me ha abierto úlceras verdes;
con un poco de cal yo me compongo
con un poco de cal y de ternura . . .

I will not fall, no, because I am strong
in vain hurricanes assail me
and time has gnawed flesh and bone
and humidity has caused green ulcers to fester;
with a little bit of plaster I will mend
with a little bit of plaster and tenderness . . .

DULCE MARIA LOYNAZ. From *Ultimos días de una casa.*
Madrid: Ediciones Torremozas, 1993. The daughter of a general in the War of Independence, Dulce María
Loynaz won the distinguished Premio Miguel de Cervantes award in 1992. She lives in Cuba.

Interior on Calle 23rd,
Havana
July 1991

ACKNOWLEDGMENTS

I would like to thank the following people for their support: my family and friends, Sam Antupit, Marilú Menéndez, Janis Lewin, Elisa Urbanelli, Adam Bartos, and Enrique Fernández.

In Cuba: with love and gratitude, I'd like to thank Daniel González and his family, Osmany Batista, his family, and the people of Agilar, Cristina and Figueroa, Alejandro Hartmann, Father Valentín Sanz, and my friends in Havana and Boyeros.

En Cuba: con cariño y agradecimiento quiero dar gracias a Daniel González y su familia, Osmany Batista, su familia y la gente de Agilar; Cristina y Figueroa, Alejandro Hartmann, Padre Valentín Sanz, y mis amigos de La Habana y Boyeros.

CREDITS

CUBA: THE ELUSIVE ISLAND was produced by CommonPlace Publishing and designed by Samuel N. Antupit. The display type is LSC Condensed, created by Tom Carnese in 1970 for International Typeface Corporation. A highly stylized face based upon Bodoni, it does not exhibit the clumsiness of that type's condensed versions. The extreme thick and thin strokes shift abruptly, reducing the geometric rigidity of the face.

The secondary display type is Bitstream's digital version of the Egiziano originally cast by the Italian Nebiolo Foundry in 1905. This bold face is typical of those in common use in the United States, England, France, and Italy during the nineteenth century. Notable for a uniformity of strokes and broad serifs, versions of these types were variously described as Egyptians, Antiques, or Clarendons but are now unceremoniously categorized as slab serifs.

The text has been set in DeVinne, one of the many designs named for Theodore DeVinne, an influential American printer, designer, and author in the late nineteenth and early twentieth centuries. This face, issued by the Linotype Corporation in 1902, is a modern roman characterized by long, thin serifs and considerable thick/thin contrast. Although the roman has an overall even texture, the swelling of the thick strokes produces a rhythmic italic.

The type for this book was digitally composed at Franklin/Lazernet in New York City. The book was printed and bound by Oddi Printing Corporation in Iceland.

GULF OF MEXICO

Puerto-Esperanza

Viñales

Dimas

PINAR
DEL RIO

La Fé

María là Gorda

ISLA DE LA JUVENTUD

Nueva Gerona

Cojimar   Santa María del Mar

HAVANA

Boyeros   MATANZAS

Varadero

Cárdenas

Playa Larga

Playa Girón

CIENFUEGOS

El Salto
del Habananilla

Trinidad

Isabela de Sagua

Sagua
la Grande

Cayo Conuco

Caibarién

SANTA
CLARA   Remedios

SANCTI
SPIRITUS